INNER THOUGHTS

INNER THOUGHTS

Poems suitable for Middle School

By Deanna Repose Oaks

INNER THOUGHTS

Cover Design by Deanna Repose Oaks
Book design by Deanna Repose Oaks
ISBN-13: 978-1-956482-06-5 (paperback)

Published by View from Room 217, LLC
www.viewfromroom217.com

Dedication

For Nikki. Without your constant complaints about the fact that I never allowed you to read my other collections of poetry due to the adult language and themes, these poems would not be what they are today. Hopefully, this book helps fill your void of middle school appropriate poetry. Thank you for inspiring me to take this project on.

Table of Contents

Inner Thoughts

Inner thoughts can be cruel sometimes
They never ask for input
They have no sounding board
They echo through your brain

Inner thoughts seem out of control all times
They pound the gas with their foot
They throw logic overboard
They race like a runaway train

Inner thoughts can be tamed many times
But only if in faith you put
Your friends and family aboard
And disallow any thought free reign

Values

My value is more
More than what I see
More than what I write
It is in what I do

But I write what I see
And what I write is what I do

My value comes from what I feel
And how I put it on paper to reveal
Inner truths to those that read
The words I write
About what I see

Baring My Soul

Baring My Soul
For all to see
Hoping my love
Flies out of me
In ways that help
All those that need
To heal, to hope
To believe
In themselves
More than not
Because I bared my soul
Holding back no thought

No Kidnap Needed

Voices blend into similar frequency
A low hummmmm not quite a buzzzzz
As the flurry of excitement passes from one to another

Watching from afar, wanting to kidnap the feeling
Hold it hostage
Keep it forever

But the buzzzz is fleeting and the hummm slowly dies
All that is left to kidnap are empty rooms
And forgotten fries

Yet the excitement remains for days
For it was given freely
Even to those afar

No kidnap needed

What's Your Name Again?

I didn't get your name
I enjoyed your smile just the same
The connection brief and fast
The exchange itself will last
Belief in me, greater from our meet
But may never find you on the street
Know that I think about you all the time
Even if you didn't say your name and I didn't say mine

Seeking Sameness

I am seeking sameness now
I was proud to be different and unlike you

And, it seems, I've just broken through
The wall I built to BE that wouldn't allow
Any such sameness I seemed to lack
Because I became different a long way back

The sameness I found is in heart and in hand
A greatness you can understand
And still, the differences will be cherished
So we can all be enriched
I am seeing sameness now

Thank you.

The Forest

I'm surrounded by trees
Taller, stronger, greater
I'm striving
To hear all they bestow
For a presence within their midst

They give me room to breathe
Part their branches
Allow me my own light
I'm quiet as I bask
In the greatness surround

Until I see the sapling
Smaller than me
I give it room
Part my branches
Give it light
I'm loud as I bestow
Because the greatness
Echoes through the trees

What I See

Looking at a tree
Seeing the forest before me
Wondering why this molehill
Is a mountain still

I've seen what the problem truly is
I can't get my imagination to dismiss
The shadow stretches through the day
Long and strong, as the sun rests from play
Darkening the doors of opportunity
Making them looked closed to me

I know this about me
Yet I can't rearrange what I see

So Can You

My voice shakes as I explain
How hard it is to speak
Not about everyday things
But those that make me weak
I work everyday to grow beyond
This obstacle of my youth
The words I write help so much
And offer you this proof
Even if I cannot speak the words
I can beat back my fear

So can you

Magic In the Mundane

I don't look for the magic in the mundane
I give my magic to the mundane
A smile to someone at the checkout line
An uplifting comment on a shirt
A compliment on a smile
A hug
It doesn't take much to cast the spell
A bit of time
A small action
A minuscule change in someone's mundane life
Can change that life forever
It can be magic
You may never know where that magic will lead them
Sometimes, it propels them to greatness
So I try to be the magic in the mundane

Love and Support

"You have done for me in the past
So I will do for you"
And as you say this, I reply
Did I really? How true?
Because I just can't believe
So much was done
Just by being a friend
As I am to everyone
But you assured me
What was said was true
"And you show your support
In all that you do"
But I still don't believe
As your actions are so rare
That what I have done
Can even compare
Then I stop and realize
This simple truth
What didn't mean all that much to me
Meant the world to you

Don't Doubt Yourself

Doubts creep and crawl through your thoughts
Like termites in the walls
Eating away the structure of your dreams
If you avoid them, the house will fall at your feet
Best to eradicate them

How do you eradicate a colony on the loose?
Pick up the phone
Call in reinforcements
A friend
A colleague
An exterminator, perhaps?
Someone that sees your worth
And can reflect it to you
So you can see the doubts for what they are
Small, little bugs eating at your dreams
Bugs that can be squashed in an instant

When you don't doubt yourself

Twinkling Lights

The lights twinkle instead of blind
The cars are ribbons intertwined
The distance is soothing to the soul
The path is defined to the goal
When viewed from afar while in the sky
Up here, dreams are left to vie

Waves

Waves of the ocean soothe your soul
But waves of anxiety put you out of control
And waves of grief curl you into a ball
When you least expect the waves at all
One minute you are flying high
Next, all you want to do is lie
Somewhere other than the space you're in
Running away from all rolling within
But the waves cling like sand beneath your feet
While standing on the beach
Digging you in deep, deeper still
Burying you in all you feel
With every wave that rolls on through
What are you supposed to do?

Swim out beyond the break
Grab the board and take
The wave from the sea
Ride it back to the beach

Seems simple on paper when the waves don't crash
Push you back into the sand
Every time you try to stand
If you can't stand, you can't swim
And the effort is beyond the available strength
Even if you could persist at length
Trying as you might, you won't move
For the sand holds your feet fast
While the waves forever last

Waves, Cont'd

Then a friend stands by your side
Tells you when there's a turn in the tide
Hands you a bigger board to surf
Gets you past the waves, off the turf

Power

I hold this gift in the palm of my hand
It's powerful, but doesn't demand
To be released
So I hold tight, keep it for me
And watch as the power dwindles
While I'm spinning yarn onto spindles
Instead of weaving into being
Strength of character...

Happiness starts fleeting
Holding tight is hurting more
Than that time, my foot in the door
I see the path so very clear
I need to share this gift dear
Share the power of light within
So others can breathe it in

Staying Out Of The Way

I've learned, through trial and error
It doesn't pay to be visible
When things go awry
Better to stick to the shadows
Or just out of the line of sight
To keep the fallout a far cry
Away

I don't hide but rather avoid
The eye of the hurricane
And the bands of the storms
Out of the rain
But somehow I still get soaked
Sometimes I wonder
Will it be better
To face the storm head on?

Concept of Time

Watches, clocks, and sundials
Decorations all
Because time doesn't matter
Not even to the clock on the wall
It speeds up, slows down
Sometimes even stands still
We can never control it
Try to overcome it, we will
But try as we might
We are doomed to fail
Because time continues to fly
No matter how loud we wail
So once we all realize
Changing time is for naught
We can stop chasing it
And live happy when time is forgot

As Pinks

Heaps of positive thoughts are
Like a white load of laundry in bleach
The whites get whiter, but they remain white
The dirt erased, never to be thought of again

A single negative thought is
Like a red sock in the white load
The red bleeds over everything
Infecting the clothes fundamentally
Forever changing them

A reminder of the red sock will persist
Every time the whites are viewed
As pinks
For their color cannot be removed once died

So Lost

The dining table of our family camper was a map

Our driver taught me to read the map before I read books
Even numbers go East West or West East
Odd numbers go North South or South North
Three numbers are connectors

Except for the 101
Which goes in all directions in more than 1 place
And only connects Los Angeles, CA to Seattle, WA

Things were simple with the map on the table
Even if you spilled soda
There was no screaming
        "recalculating route" or "turn left now"
From a horrid machine still not hip that a fork is not a turn
It is a utensil used to stab hot dogs off paper plates
while avoiding mosquitoes

Signs above the freeways were matched
Between the map and the road
Distance was measured with sticky fingers
        and map legends
And completed math equations determined
        when we would arrive

"If driving at 55 mph for 100 miles, how long will it take to
        get there?"
Was 100/55/60, not a time stamp subject to change when
        crossing time zones

So Lost, Cont'd

There was no location determined with a "re-center" icon
There were only cities such as San Jose
   not San Joe-see
And Lompoc with a short o and a long o
not Lom-pock like the wine drinkers say

Toll roads were marked with dashes
   not pictures of Mickey Mouse
Lakes and rivers were blue lines or dots
   or squiggly shapes hard to define
Unless they were state lines
Like Kentucky, Illinois, Ohio, South Carolina

Mississippi defining more than the longest border
"K"'s or the "W"'s on the dials of radios and TVs

Yet, my phone died the other day,
   and I couldn't find my way home
Even though the map is still on the table in the camper
The camper is long gone
The driver isn't driving anymore
And I'm so lost

Eyesight

I don't see things like you
You see surface; I see through
What wouldn't waste your time
Becomes cherished when mine
All those people, disregarded
I see them as brokenhearted
Please stop, stay awhile
See beyond their rank and file
Enjoy the world and the beauty within
Before your end begins

Story To Tell

I want to write a story
But I don't know which to tell
Should I recant my broken heart
Or the time I fell
I don't know what makes you happy
Or what makes you mad
I don't know what will make you think
Or what will make you glad
I sit and ponder all my words
Instead of writing them down
Afraid, as always
The story will make you frown
So the stories remain untold
As if they never were
And each day goes by faster
In a story-less blur

Lap Blankets

I made this gift full of love
Laid it in a box
Wrapped it up in pretty paper
Put a bow on top
Gave it to you on that day
You met me with a sneer
"Get that away from me
I cannot have it here"
As I watched you toss it away
My heart filled with dread
Because I knew what happened next
Upon the box you tread
Now I carry the ruined box
Instead of the love inside
Because I chose to give my gift
To someone impolite

Kitty Cuddle Time

Relaxing on my recliner
Under my lap blanket
Thinking of the love
Within all the layers
My cats can't stay away
They revel in the warmth
Curl at my feet
Lay across my stomach
I want to think its me
They appear for
But I know it is the blanket
Because when it isn't there
Neither are they
I accept their truth
And use the blanket
Even in a heat wave
For the love they infuse grows stronger
With every kitty cuddle

Mind of a Cat

Let me in, I want your bed
Quick now, I want to be fed
Sleep here on the stair
Step over me, I don't care
Please clean the litter now
Otherwise I poop on the couch
Lay down on the floor
Wait, did you want to open the door?
Too bad, I'm comfy here
Please go away dear
Quick, I want to be fed
Let me in, I want your bed

Figuring It Out

I miss the days of 1 on 1
Before there was an algorithm
To tell me what to watch
What to buy
What to listen to
I miss the days of being lost
Before there was a voice
To tell me where to go
Which accidents to avoid
Where the cops were watching
There was more fun in the unknown
More fun in finding different from what I like
The wrong turns
I miss the challenge of ...
Of thinking, trying, failing, and
Falling in love with something
I figured out

Just For Me

Some things are just for me
Especially the giggles
That erupt from thoughts
Unrelated to time and place
Just for me
Not about you
Or for you
Or involving you
Even when you and I are alone
Memories of a line from a book
Read long ago
Or a lyric from a song
Some fleeting thought
Where giggles ensued
Trust me, not about you

Heartfelt And True

I want to offer up something
. . .
But my heart isn't in it
I want to feel something
. . .
But my heart can't take it
I want to believe something
. . .
But my heart won't allow it

Because . . . eroded
By impostors and lies
My heart is now hardened
Because of the disguise
I want to trust again
I truly do
Because I loved life
When it was . . .

(hint: replace . . . with the title of this poem and read it again)

Seeking Direction

I use circumstances
To circumvent
Almost running a circus
Like Ringling Bros

But end up in Indianapolis
Racing around in circles
With each new circumstance
Circling around again

I want to change direction
But I never stay in one
Long enough to know
In which direction I need to go

Hocus Focus

I'm focusing on the stupid stuff
The book in the background
Instead of the person in the fore
The spine is so clear
The breaks in the binding
Displays where it is broken
To fix it I must
I refocus the shot
To capture it anew
Trying to bring focus
To ...
Yet the person still blends, is all fuzzy
And the book is again center stage
Even though it is unimportant
And can be disregarded
I refocus, again and again
Hoping the picture adjusts
To put the book in the background
And the person in the fore
But somehow the book always wins

By 1

I don't add
But I also don't subtract
I multiply by 1
Or by -1
To create positivity
Enhancing situations
With presence

Overfeeling

I'm family but I feel
I'm way too far away
Can't do much
Can't extend my stay
My guilt grows
With every passing day
I'm family so they feel
My love even from beyond the bay

Sleepwalking

Got out of bed
Still wanting sleeps
Somehow lost time
Even though my phone beeps
Reminders of tasks
Yet to be done
Deep breath in
Task list be won

Lines To Escape

There is a green line
A blue line
A white line
A red line
And stations filled with people
Speakers blaring announcements overhead

I long for the train
To whisk me away
Somewhere past where the green line ends
The green hills

I long for the train
To whisk me away
Somewhere where the blue line ends
The ocean waters

I long for the train
To whisk me away
Somewhere where the white line ends
The gentle fog

I long for the train
To whisk me away
Somewhere past where the red line ends

But incessant beeps
Interrupt the longing

Powering Down

Mending my heart
Is just the start
My head must become clear
Rid of overshadowing fear
So I'm again keeping quiet
Better than having to hide it

No Words Today

Can't seem to write the words
Or find the photo
To express my socials

My heart is elsewhere
Close to family
Reconnecting in person
With love and light
So forgive my social absence today

Falling Down

Falling down, skinning my knee
Getting up, afraid to be
Doing what I just did
So now, the time, I bid

Fear grows over time
As reflections of falling remind
Of all the things done wrong

But there is a way to do it right
Get up, continue to fight
Learn from my mistakes
Grow beyond, raise the stakes
Brush off the grime and dirt
Do it again, avoid getting hurt
So I can sing a victory song

No Traction

My wheels are stuck dead
The tires, brand new, with deep tread
All weather, still spin in the crud
Snow in the winter, but other times mud
I've tried tools, rocks, salt
Still stuck, still my fault
I drove this car here, with directions
From friends, foes, misconceptions
I've pushed, I've pulled, I've used chains
And still no ground has gained

I've added weights, deflated tires
Screamed, yelled, lit fires
I've stripped it bare for all to see
Still stuck, look, can't you help me?
The answer is no more oft than not
Because I put myself here, caught

Between the dream I thought I chased
And this huge, colossal mistake
Of thinking people were like me
And would assist my dream to be
But every time I turn around
I'm torn apart and run aground

Woke Up Late

Woke up late, no minutes to spare
Unset alarm did not blare
Loud enough for me to hear the time was now
To rise from depths of dreams, start my day somehow
Getting dressed in a rush
Where is my missing brush
Wait, I need to eat
And put shoes on my feet
Ask myself, am I forgetting something?
Oh, yeah, my phone, with the alarm that didn't ring

Time Lapse

I got so wrapped in the moment that time slipped away
I didn't notice the seconds, the minutes, the hours, the day
Blinders on, completing the tasks at hand
Forever moving forward, toward the demand
Yet, I'm still lost within this vortex
Of a system too complex
That the gears of the clock will not unwind
And I will never reclaim my lost time
Not that I would, even if I could,
For the moment was worth it in every way.

Emotional Release

My emotions are on these pages
Left unread beyond my last breath
Emotions spilled in moments and ages
Left there to die a death
My release eases my pain
Right before it surges ahead
It ebbs but does not completely wane
Right after I put it to bed
My emotional release twists my feel
From pain and anger to something real
Hope grows from each word
Even if they remain unheard

Even if they remain unheard
Hope grows from each word
From pain and anger to something real
My emotional release twists my feel
Right after I put it to bed
It ebbs but does not completely wane
Right before it surges ahead
My release eases my pain
Left there to die a death
Emotions spilled in moments and ages
Left unread beyond my last breath
My emotions are on these pages

Pigeon Holed

Pigeon holed is how I feel
With labels that give me:
> gender
> color
> religion
> height
> weight
> size
> clothing
> politics
> or lack thereof

I do not fit and never will
Because I'm me and strong willed
I cannot be defined with simple pronouns
Give me a label if you must
I will just reassign something greater for myself
To the ways I know and love
Whatever
Never-mind

Last Day

As the sun sets below the horizon
The sky fills with colors unsurpassed
The crickets start chattering
And the fireflies alight
I spend these moments with you
Hoping to keep from expressing my fear

I take solace from silence between us
And the shared knowledge
That soon the sun will rise again
With a brilliance greater than sunset
And skies bluer than most
Knowing that in the darkness
The earth is still solid beneath my feet

At least for now

Hopefully tomorrow we'll be able to share it again

Friends

I think of my friends often
Even the ones I don't see each day
I always hope they're good
And living in their best way
Sometimes I reach out
Sometimes I forget

My love for them
Is there when they're in need
Just as I know
They are there for me
Sometimes they reach out
Sometimes they forget

Yet, even if years go by
Without a word
They are my friends
Most deserved

Contradictory

Meaning one thing, saying another
Wanting you to understand both
At the same time
But each are contradictory
Canceling out both the feeling and the action
Always, leaving me wanting more
To explain more, to learn more at the same time
To read you while turning a blind eye
Still so contradictory
And wanting...
Explaining the one thing, telling another

Black Cherry Soda

The journey began with a quest
To fill a Styrofoam cup with a soda
Sounds simple enough
Until the journey begins
The road stretches before us
Getting longer with every mile driven
Cars speeding by, cutting us off, braking
Too fast, too slow, never just right
Entrance ramps, exchanges, ladders in the road
Favorite song on the radio
Played too loud, not loud enough
Then, up ahead the sign
EXIT NOW

Black Cherry Soda

A taste from childhood
A new memory made
A quest won
Yet the journey isn't over
The road still stretches before us
Although the miles are now familiar
The dangers still lurk
More so now than before
Cars multiplied while braking and speeding
Cones appeared with flashing lights and blocked lanes
There is no sign at the end of EXIT NOW
No quest to be won upon arrival
Just survival

Sad Sky

I looked up to the sky
Beheld the sight
Of gray skies covering black
With pops of blue in the back
Grabbed my camera and thought
Please stay still enough to be caught

Every shade of sadness here
Without a raindrop near
Gives me hope that there will be
A day ahead, full of possibility
If the sky can move with these colors bright
There is a chance that I just might
Move from dark cloud to blue sky
In just a blink of an eye
And even if I blink twice
The sky above will remind me trice
I can be dark, gray, and blue
All at once, every hue
Just like the sky above today.

Hummingbirds & Bees

I flit from flower to flower
Never staying too long
At the flower's side
I'm flitting too fast for that
Because there is always a better flower
Just over there
Flit, flit, flit
Always onto the new
Yet, I love all the flowers that sustain
And remember each in its way

Beg to differ, but you are not a hummingbird
Flitting from flower to flower
You were never meant to stay for long
At the flower's side
You are moving at the proper pace
Because the flowers are in need
Just over there
Buzz, Buzz, Buzz
Always onto the broken
Pollinating the flowers with sustenance
Breathing life into each in your way

Tug of War

I'm the rope in a tug of war
Frayed ends held taut
A marker dividing my length by half
Stretched thin by force
Held in place by weight
And counterweight
Suspended above reprieve
Wrapped along the arms of both teams who have
Entrenched themselves
In a battle not easily won
Salvation can only be celebrated
Once a team lets go
Or falls down
Yet neither will relinquish their hold

Memory Lane

Watching old movies
Hearing old songs
Transports to time & place
Memories magnified
Sharp corners rounded with time
Shading pain of today
While reliving yesterdays
Doesn't keep me present

Beliefs

Are they chosen
Or thrust upon us?
Do we always have them
Or do they appear?
Can we change them
Or are they ingrained?
Why do we follow them
Or can we disregard?
If we believe today
What happens when we disbelieve tomorrow?
Are they gone forever
Or will they come back?

Sinking In

I need to let everything sink in
The theme of the story I just read
It made me angry, hurt my feelings
Then, it made me dread

It seemed to check all the boxes
But there was a story to tell
Yet I still felt empty
As I wanted to yell

My inner turmoil is thriving
After I've reached the end
I wrestled with the text
And the money spend

Now that the book is closed
I'm trying to let it all sink in
I believe I'll have a better heart
Than I did before I begin

Messy Mind

I cannot pick up the puzzle pieces from the floor
There are too many colors
There is no discernible pattern
Even if the pieces are the same color
The shapes are all squiggly
Not the same
Some are upside down
The right side up ones don't fit together
Did someone put these here like this purposefully?
Maybe I should pick them up
Order them
Discover the pattern
Yeah, I'll leave them alone
Walk around them
Or over them
Look at them everyday
Wonder when that someone will come along
and fix this mess
Because I'm sure it was someone else
I'd never just toss the pieces like this
So un orderly
No, I need to fix this
But how do I start?
Will I upset someone??

Messy Mind, Cont'd

...

If so, I don't want to anger them
Anger is no good
It has been so long, is there even a someone?
Sometimes No One is the culprit
Sometimes every one is
Sometimes it is me
Maybe I'll stand guard, ask everyone
Ask no one

...

What am I standing here for?
And who left these pieces laying here?

Monday

Is in the wrong place in my calendar
It bothers me so
I cannot get my week straight
I do not know
Coffee doesn't do the trick
Neither does tea
As I start my week ahead
Tasks double indubitably

Then the fires start
Can't put them out
People desire more attention
Cause so much doubt
All the while I want to go to bed
And sleep a little more
Because Monday is where my Sunday was
On the calendar I had before

Feeling BLAH

Trying to put a smile in my voice
As I answer the phone
Even though all I want is solitude
And to stay at home

Trying to put a smile on my face
As I greet my friend
Even though all I want is quiet
And this party's end

Trying to put energy in my dance
As I reach the floor
Even though all I want is stillness
And the other side of the door

Trying to put energy in my BLAH
As my thoughts grow dark
Even though all I see is the light
Of your amazing spark

Succeeding to put thanks into my hugs
As you lift my spirits
Because getting me out of myself
Keeps my BLAH where I can't hear it

Sarcastic Voice

That was my sarcastic voice
But you wouldn't know
My delivery is too fast
Your pick up is too slow

You begin to hate me
And all that I say
My delivery so dry
The opposite convey

How long did you know me
Before you could see
The sarcastic dry wit
That is basically me?

10 years? 15?

A single phone call
Changed your view
You laughed so hard
I didn't know what to do

"I get it now, you are so funny
All this time, I disliked you so
But now I hear all the jokes
You've told since long ago"

That call changed my life
Became such a happy place
Instead of the scowl you always wore
There was a smile in its place

Monday Blues Strike Again

I'm not getting out
Take me home
I'd rather be in bed

I love my job
I really do
Yeah, that's what I said

Yesterday was better
Even running around
Stuff got done

Today the grind
Is back against the wheel
There isn't any fun

Stress from driving
To the job I have
Looking to be paid

But all I want
Is my cozy bed
Where I wish I stayed

I Just Can't

I want to wake up cheery
Like those bubbly people I know

I want to fulfill my plans
Like those successful people I know

I want my work to be complete
Like those satisfied people I know

I want to be friendly
Like those popular people I know

I just can't

Not today
Too much too early
Maybe my can't will make it better
(But will probably make it worse)

I want to go back to bed
Nix my plans
Abandon work
Keep to myself

I just can't
Because today
Is the only day I CAN
        So I do, even though I don't want to

Tedium

I got lost in the forest
So many trees
Spent all of my days
Picking up leaves

I got lost in the house
So many frills
Spent all of my days
Paying the bills

I got lost in the store
So many questions
Spent all of my days
Practicing concessions

I got lost in the car
So many mad dashes
Spent all of my days
Praying against crashes

I am now so very lost
I cannot find myself
So I'm asking you
"Please get me out of this"

Spring Blooms

It comes from the trees
It floats on the breeze
It makes me wheeze

Grab my inhaler, quick
The air is just too thick
I think I'm about to die

The meds help, but don't heal
Another round, another wheal
Why did I want this deal?

I feel so much better now
I breathe without inhalers somehow

Oh, wait, it's winter

Another season started yesterday
Two months too soon I say
Make it go away
Please!

Twisting Words

There they are all in the book
Strung together haphazardly
Waiting for someone
To reveal their worth

Sometimes impatient like people
Waiting for validation
Approval of others
They are words

Just like all the other words in all the other books
But different somehow
For their order, poignant
Their in-order more so

The reader can twist them
However they please, or not
To prove a point
Disprove a theory
Build someone up
Take someone down

Soft as a flower on a cool spring day
Sharper than a sword at the neck of a king
Words... strung together haphazardly
In a book
Waiting for you

Author's Note

Hello! As mentioned in the dedication, this book was inspired by Nikki, who at the time it was written attended sixth grade. She not only complained enough for me to hear her, but she also helped curate, and/or inspire, several of these poems. Her insight into these words has forever changed me – for the better.

I've always had a hard time finding editors for my poetry, mostly because the editors I tried using never saw eye to eye on my style. I tend to avoid punctuation because I feel my words have a natural rhyme and rhythm all their own. I don't rhyme on PURPOSE all that much, yet most of my poems rhyme. With that said, I'd like to thank Bridget for being the teacher she is. She got carried away and edited my work as if I was a fifth-grade student submitting homework. The insight she provided strengthened many of the poems. While I couldn't elevate her into the dedication, know she is in these words as much as she's in my heart.

I am still in awe that Tricia felt Waves, Don't Doubt Yourself, Falling Down, and Mind of a Cat were strong enough to be included in her 6th grade poetry lesson. Adding me to the classroom poetry pennant put me on the wall with some amazing poets and I am truly humbled. This meant more to me than having my books on the shelf at Barnes & Noble next to Edgar Allan Poe, because this time it wasn't alphabetical order that put me there, it was strength.

Jessica, thanks again for being my hero. Your comments throughout the rough draft helped me see my work through your eyes and heart, which really balanced out the editing process for me. I am now swinging for the fences!

I posted some of the poems included in this book on my Facebook page. Every posted poem had a cheerleader named Phyllis. She started cheering me on after claiming she didn't like poetry. Changing her mind made me realize these poems aren't half bad, even before they were shared around the world.
(https://www.facebook.com/deannareposeoaks).

Jennifer, thank you for your insight into my work, not just this book, but the last two as well. I spend so much time alone with my words, discussing them with you makes me understand the effort to write them is not a wasted endeavor.

To anyone and everyone who reads my words, thank you for allowing me to share my feelings with you. It is not easy sharing feelings, but when we share, burdens lift and understanding broadens, not just from the person sharing them, but for all involved. Thank you for being involved.

c